JERUSALEM OR DEATH

Palestinian TERRORISM

Samuel M. KATZ

Lerner Publications Company/Minneapolis

To the heroes of ESU who saved the
Borough of Kings that fateful night in 1997
—SMK

Publisher's Note: The information in this book was current at the time of publication. However, the publisher is aware that news involving current events dates quickly. Please refer to the websites on page 69 for places to go to obtain up-to-date information.

Lerner Publications Company
A division of Lerner Publishing Group
241 First Avenue North
Minneapolis, Minnesota U.S.A.

Website address: www.lernerbooks.com

Library of Congress Cataloging-in-Publication Data

Katz, Samuel M., 1963–
        Jerusalem or death : Palestinian terrorism / by Samuel M. Katz.
           p.   cm. — (Terrorist dossiers)
        Summary: Surveys historical and current events in the Palestinian-Israeli conflict, within the disputed areas and beyond, including the origins, goals, and activities of the major movements and groups.
        Includes bibliographical references and index.
        ISBN: 0–8225–4033–9 (lib. bdg. : alk. paper)
        1. Arab-Israeli conflict—Juvenile literature. [1. Arab-Israeli conflict. 2. Terrorism—Palestine.] I. Title: Palestinian terrorism. II. Title.
     DS119.7.K327 2004
     956.9405—dc21   2003006451

Manufactured in the United States of America
1 2 3 4 5 6 – DP – 09 08 07 06 05 04

CONTENTS

INTRODUCTION

The shaky news footage and grainy photographs are still haunting more than thirty years later. The camera focuses on a single Palestinian terrorist. Wearing a ski mask, the slender male figure stands on a balcony in Munich, a city in what was then West Germany. In the apartment behind him, his partners guard nine terrified Israeli hostages. And around the world, glued to their television sets, millions of people watch and wait.

The masked terrorist on a Munich balcony *(top)* became the most powerful symbol of terrorism for a whole generation. A negotiator speaks to another of the terrorists *(bottom)*.

The chilling drama began on September 5, 1972, ten days into the Munich Summer Olympics. Early that morning, Palestinian terrorists struck without warning, killing two members of the Israeli Olympic team and taking nine others hostage. The world watched breathlessly as negotiations began to free the captive Israeli athletes. But the talks went nowhere. Later known as the Munich Olympic Massacre, the standoff ended less than twenty-four hours after it had begun, culminating in a desperate gun battle on an airport tarmac—and the terrorists' execution of the remaining nine Israeli hostages.

Since the early twentieth century, Palestinians and Jews have struggled to live on the same hotly contested strip of Middle Eastern land. For more than fifty years, terrorist groups operating in the name of the liberation of Palestine have waged a nearly continuous conflict targeting the State of Israel and its allies, including nations such as the United States and others that have supported the Jewish state. The terrorists' goal is to achieve the establishment of an independent state for the Palestinian people. In Munich they sought to demonstrate to the world that some Palestinians were ready and willing to commit acts of unspeakable horror to achieve that goal.

That masked figure in Munich remains one of the symbols of Palestinian terrorism. To some, he stands for the bitter tragedy of the Palestinian people. To others, he represents the brutal and bloody attacks that Palestinian terrorist groups have carried out against Israeli citizens. The bloodshed from the conflict has been horrific on both sides. The suffering has been indescribable. And this devastating terrorist war shows no signs of ending.

Abu Nidal Organization: a terrorist group founded by
Sabri al-Banna (Abu Nidal) in the 1980s

anti-Semitism: discrimination against or hostility toward Jews

al-Aqsa Martyrs Brigades: a terrorist force formed by
Fatah commanders in 2000

Arab Liberation Front (ALF): an Iraqi-supported terrorist
faction formed in 1969 and led by Abdul Rahim Ahmed

Yasser Arafat: a leader within the Palestine Liberation
Organization and figurehead of the Palestinian cause

Balfour Declaration: a 1917 letter from British statesman
Arthur James Balfour to Zionist leader Lord Lionel Walter
Rothschild. It declared British support for the creation of a
Jewish state from the British mandate of Palestine, provided
that the non-Jewish population retained its freedoms and rights.

B.C.E. and C.E.: Middle Eastern history spans both ancient
and modern times. To refer to historical dates, some books
use the abbreviations B.C. ("before Christ") and A.D.
("anno Domini," or "in the year of the Lord") to date
events. This dating system is based on the birth of Jesus.
This book uses an alternative method—B.C.E., or "before the
common era," instead of B.C., and C.E., or "of the common
era," instead of A.D.

Black September Organization: a terrorist group and
special operations force founded in 1971 by Fatah
commanders and named after a 1970 attack on Palestinian
refugee camps in Jordan

Democratic Front for the Liberation of Palestine (DFLP): a terrorist group founded in 1969 by Nayef Hawatmeh

Diaspora: the Jewish population outside of Israel

Fatah: one of the oldest Palestinian terrorist militias, founded by Yasser Arafat and Khalil Wazir in the 1950s

fedayeen: Palestinian militants organized into armed groups to attack Israeli citizens and interests

George Habash: founder of the Popular Front for the Liberation of Palestine

Hamas: a militant Islamic terrorist group founded by Sheikh Ahmed Yassin in 1987

intifada: a broad Palestinian uprising, largely carried out by civilians rather than terrorist factions

Islam: a religion founded on the Arabian Peninsula in the seventh century C.E. by the prophet Muhammad. The religion's primary tenets are known as the Five Pillars of Islam, and its holy book is the Quran.

Israel Defense Forces (IDF): Israel's primary security and military organization

Israeli government: the authority that has been targeted by Palestinian terrorists and that has mobilized various forces to combat terrorism

Ahmed Jibril: founder and commander of the Popular Front for the Liberation of Palestine General Command

Judaism: a religion that began to evolve in the Middle East close to four thousand years ago. The faith's primary tenets are contained in a holy text called the Torah.

Mossad: Israel's foreign intelligence counterterrorist unit

Palestine Liberation Front (PLF): an Iraqi-sponsored terrorist group founded in the late 1970s and led by Muhammad Abbas (Abu Abbas)

Palestine Liberation Organization (PLO): an umbrella group founded in 1964 to represent Palestinian movements. The PLO is regarded by some observers as legitimate and by others as a terrorist organization.

Palestinian Islamic Jihad (PIJ): a militant Islamic terrorist group founded in about 1980 by Fathi Shaqaqi

Popular Front for the Liberation of Palestine (PFLP): a terrorist group founded in late 1967 by Dr. George Habash

Popular Front for the Liberation of Palestine General Command (PFLP-GC): a terrorist group founded in 1968 by Ahmed Jibril and supported by Syria and Iran

rejectionists: Palestinian groups or individuals who, with the goal of an independent Palestinian state, view any and all compromise with Israel as unacceptable

Shin Bet: Israel's domestic intelligence and counterintelligence force

Tanzim: a terrorist militia formed in 1995 by Fatah

UN Resolution 242: a UN resolution passed in 1967 after the Six-Day War

Zionism: an international political movement, founded by Theodor Herzl in the late 1800s, to establish a Jewish homeland in the area that became the modern State of Israel

A HISTORICAL TAPESTRY

At the center of the Palestinian-Israeli conflict is one issue: two peoples claiming ownership to the same sliver of land. Covering no more than 10,500 square miles, the region in question borders the Jordan River to the east, the Mediterranean Sea to the west, the Sinai Peninsula to the south, and the Lebanese frontier to the north. Intensifying the conflict is the fact that, for some of the parties involved, it is also a religious war pitting Islam against Judaism.

THE SONS OF ABRAHAM

Jewish ties to what is often called the Promised Land date back nearly four thousand years. According to the Torah, one of Judaism's holy documents, God promised Abraham and the Hebrews land in Canaan in the 1700s B.C.E. Abraham gathered his people, settled among the Canaanites, and raised a family in his new home. Twelve of his descendants came to be known as the fathers of the twelve tribes of

Israel and the disputed territories lie at the heart of the Middle East.

Israel. One of these twelve—Judah—would give his name to Judaism, the religion of the Hebrews.

In the 1100s B.C.E., a people called the Philistines—whom modern Palestinians claim as their ancestors—settled along Canaan's southern coast. Over the next few centuries, the Philistines pushed eastward and eventually encroached on the land of the Jews. The two groups clashed, and, led by King David, the Jews defeated the Philistines in a decisive war.

David's son Solomon succeeded him in the 900s B.C.E. During his reign, the Beit ha-Mikdash (the First Holy Temple) was built in Jerusalem, the Jews' holy city.

While it thrived economically and culturally, the Jewish realm began to weaken militarily and proved no match for invading armies. In 586 B.C.E., Babylonian invaders demolished the First Temple, destroying an important symbol of Jewish religion, culture, and political strength. A Second Temple was built on the same site in 515 B.C.E. However, the invasions continued. As conquerors took control, the Jews were often exiled to faraway lands. But many of them eventually returned to the land that they believed had been bestowed upon them by God.

Many Jewish holy documents are written in Hebrew script.

When the Roman Empire conquered Israel in 63 B.C.E., Roman leaders gave Jewish communities some autonomy. However, in 70 C.E., Jewish revolts against Roman rule spurred the Romans to demolish the Second Temple and force the Jews into exile once more. These exiles, who journeyed to distant European and Asian lands, became known as the Jewish Diaspora. The deep yearning of exiled Jews to return to Jerusalem and their Jewish homeland became the cornerstone of Jewish prayers—and of Jewish political activism.

THE CALL OF THE PROPHET

Meanwhile, the region remained under Roman rule. In the 300s C.E., the emperor Constantine adopted Christianity as the official faith of the Roman Empire, and the young religion had thousands of followers. Jerusalem, as the site of important events in the life of Jesus (the central figure of Christianity), became a sacred city to Christians as well as Jews.

In about 610, the religion of Islam was founded by Muhammad, an Arab merchant from Mecca (a city in modern Saudi Arabia). Muhammad's revelations from God (Allah, in Arabic) were recorded in the Quran, Islam's holy text. But the faith's rise was slow at first, and Muhammad encountered such hostility from followers of existing religions that he left Mecca for nearby Medina.

Muhammad found a following in Medina, and Islam grew swiftly thereafter. In the mid- to late 600s, Islamic warriors swept across the Middle East and the Arab world, taking hold of what by then was known as Palestine. Mosques—places of Islamic worship—sprang up throughout the region. In 691 a sacred shrine called the Dome of the Rock was built on the site where the Second Temple had stood. Muslims (followers of Islam) believed that the spot was where Prophet Muhammad had slept on

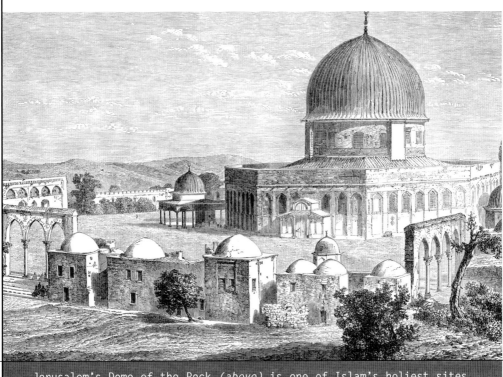

Jerusalem's Dome of the Rock *(above)* is one of Islam's holiest sites.

Christian Crusaders invade Jerusalem in 1099. The Dome of the Rock is visible in the background.

his journey to heaven. The al-Aqsa Mosque was built just south of the Dome of the Rock. Muslims soon came to view Jerusalem as the third holiest place in Islam, after the cities of Mecca and Medina.

But for centuries, this coveted region remained a battlefield. From the 1000s through the 1200s, it was seized by European Crusaders who sought to reclaim Jerusalem in the name of Christianity. Then the Mamluks, Islamic warriors, took control in the 1300s and 1400s. In 1516 the Ottoman Turks founded a great empire that included Palestine.

| THE DIASPORA AND THE DREAM OF ZION |

In the Diaspora—especially in Europe—Jews suffered oppression and persecution. Out of centuries of anti-Semitism grew the idea of Zion—the return to a homeland in Israel. Jews gradually began to act on the dream, trickling back to their ancient homeland. Then, in 1896, the Hungarian journalist Theodor Herzl published *Der Judenstaat (The Jews' State)*, calling for the establishment of a Jewish state. Modern Zionism was born.

Theodor Herzl

Throughout the late 1800s and early 1900s, thousands of Jews immigrated to Palestine. The Ottoman Turks, who still controlled the region, permitted Jewish immigrants to purchase land and organize agricultural settlements called kibbutzim. Kibbutzim sprang up alongside Arab towns and villages, and by 1903, approximately ten thousand Jewish settlers were living in Palestine. As the population grew, tensions arose between the newcomers and the native Palestinian Arabs, who felt threatened by the influx.

| INTERNATIONAL TIDES |

During World War I (1914–1918), Jews in Palestine supported Britain and the Allies against the Ottoman Turks. In return, the British government issued the "Balfour Declaration," pledging British support for a Jewish homeland in Palestine. But Arab residents had helped the British too, and the Arab nations were promised independence following the war. British support of both the Zionists and of Arab independence did not make a good match.

Foreign Office,
November 2nd, 1917.

Dear Lord Rothschild,

I have much pleasure in conveying to you, on behalf of His Majesty's Government, the following declaration of sympathy with Jewish Zionist aspirations which has been submitted to, and approved by, the Cabinet

"His Majesty's Government view with favour the establishment in Palestine of a national home for the Jewish people, and will use their best endeavours to facilitate the achievement of this object, it being clearly understood that nothing shall be done which may prejudice the civil and religious rights of existing non-Jewish communities in Palestine, or the rights and political status enjoyed by Jews in any other country"

I should be grateful if you would bring this declaration to the knowledge of the Zionist Federation.

Sir Arthur James Balfour *(above)* wrote the Balfour Declaration *(right)* to Zionist leader Lord Lionel Walter Rothschild on November 2, 1917.

British soldiers stand guard in Jerusalem. Throughout the 1930s, violence among Arab, Jewish, and British residents became more common.

After the Allies won the war, Great Britain and its ally France set up colonies and protectorates (dependent states) in the region. A mandate (an order granted by the international peacekeeping organization the League of Nations) gave the British control of Palestine and its inhabitants—both Jewish and Arab. But powerful nationalistic feelings rose in both the Palestinian and the Zionist camps, and fighting between Palestinians and Jews became commonplace.

Friction worsened with the rise to power of Adolf Hitler and the Nazi Party in Germany. Aggressive anti-Semitism was at the core of Nazism, and tens of thousands of Jews in Germany and nearby nations fled to Palestine as the threat of war in Europe loomed. Massive immigration of European Jews swelled Palestine's Jewish population from 174,000 in 1931 to 384,000 in 1936. Palestinian Arabs once again felt their way of life threatened. Seeking to end both British control and Jewish immigration, hundreds of Palestinians took part in strikes, riots, and attacks against British and Jewish targets in what erupted into the Palestinian Arab Revolt of 1936–1939. The revolt took place in cities such as Jerusalem, in the region of Galilee, and in rural areas.

The Palestinian Arab Revolt

Nighttime was terrifying in the Galilee area, northeast of the city of Haifa. Daylight witnessed relatively harmless workers' strikes and boycotts, staged by Arab Palestinians indignant at Jewish immigration and fearing the loss of what they, too, saw as their homeland. Sometimes these protests erupted into violent riots. And, once darkness fell, marauding gangs of Arabs ruled the roadways, attacking military vehicles, assassinating police officers, and blowing up British and Jewish targets. Others simply took advantage of the chaos, looting whatever they could find.

The Jewish kibbutzim—usually isolated and at least an hour's drive from the nearest British troops—were the main targets for the most violent groups. The attacks came quickly. Marauders slipped

Peaceful kibbutzim *(top)* were thrown into chaos and terror during the Palestinian Arab Revolt. Jewish forces *(above)* fought to defend the settlements from attack.

silently through the kibbutz fencing, avoiding guards and barbed wire. Creeping carefully through the farm, the gang, usually about twenty strong, split up and attacked houses and barns. Anyone found inside the homes—women, children, or men—was butchered with daggers or axes. Torture and rape were commonplace. The marauders were determined to leave grisly scenes in their wake that would spread tales of terror through the horrified Jewish community. Whatever could be stolen in such an attack—wheat, tractors, even sheep and cattle—was hurried back to the nearest Arab village. Whatever couldn't be taken was burned. By the time the British army arrived on the scene, the kibbutz members were busy burying the dead.

■ ■

Hoping to stop the violence, Britain decided to curb Jewish immigration to Palestine at the onset of World War II (1939–1945). British leaders planned to deal with the complicated situation after the war. But the Holocaust—in which the Nazis murdered six million European Jews in brutal death camps—changed everything. Following the war, as nations and their leaders dealt with the horrors of the Holocaust and the plight of Europe's Jews, world opinion strongly backed the Zionist call for the establishment of a Jewish state. Jewish survivors of the Holocaust were smuggled into Palestine, often slipping right past naval blockades that had been set up, in part, to prevent immigration. In response, Palestinian acts of violence increased. At the same time, Jewish terrorist groups sprang up. The most active was the Irgun Zvai Leumi, led by Menachem Begin. The Irgun carried out attacks against both Arab and British targets. On July 22, 1946, Irgun operatives planted a bomb at Jerusalem's King David Hotel, Britain's military and administrative headquarters in the region. The attack killed more than ninety people and injured dozens more.

Overwhelmed by the turmoil in Palestine, Britain decided to turn over the thorny issue to the United Nations. The United Nations was a newly formed international organization for handling global disputes.

On November 29, 1947, the United Nations voted to partition (split) Palestine into two independent states—one Jewish, the other Arab. The Jews of Palestine welcomed the UN partition and its promise of a

Jewish survivors of the Holocaust arrive in British-held Palestine
on the ship *Exodus* in 1947.

state in their ancient homeland. Native Palestinians, however, vehemently opposed the plan. They viewed Jewish claims to the land as illegitimate and feared that Jews would simply replace the British as rulers. Palestinian leaders refused any territorial compromise.

Neighboring Arab states, having recently won their independence from colonial powers, also rejected the proposal. Nevertheless, according to the UN plan, the British mandate of Palestine would end, and the Jewish State of Israel would be declared, on May 14, 1948. War seemed imminent. On May 15, thousands of Arab troops—from Egypt, Iraq, Syria, Jordan, Lebanon, Yemen, and Saudi Arabia—invaded the new nation. These troops were joined by thousands of Palestinians who, affiliated with no army, simply grabbed weapons and headed into battle. They faced off against the new and largely inexperienced Israeli army, many members of which were still recovering from the Holocaust.

Reports vary widely on the number of troops and the quality of arms on each side of the 1948 War. Some state that the Israelis were vastly outnumbered, while others assert that forces on the two sides

Israeli soldiers *(above left)* prepare to launch a mortar shell during the 1948 War. Palestinian Arabs *(above right)* defend the Jerusalem railway station. "Jerusalem" is written above the door in English, Arabic, and Hebrew.

were quite evenly matched. Whatever the figures, Israeli troops counterattacked with surprising force. Egypt captured the Gaza Strip (a narrow stretch of territory along the Mediterranean), and Jordanian fighters took the West Bank of the Jordan River. But at the end of the war, Israel held more territory than it had originally been given by the UN partition.

With Israel's territorial gains, more than 700,000 Palestinians were suddenly living in Israeli territory. Determined not to live in the Jewish state, many left their homes voluntarily. Others left out of the fear that the lingering hostilities of the war might put their lives in danger. They moved into crowded refugee camps on the West Bank, in the Gaza Strip, Lebanon, Syria, and Jordan.

One war was over. But with the anger and despair of thousands of Palestinians seething in the refugee camps, no one knew if the violence would end too.

STIRRINGS OF VIOLENCE:
EARLY GROUPS

The Palestinians who had flooded into temporary camps after the 1948 War were stateless refugees. Their rights to work, travel, and gain citizenship were limited. Palestinian discontent and despair soon took shape in the form of armed militants called *fedayeen*, meaning "men of sacrifice." Egypt, which held the Gaza Strip, organized some of these groups to launch hit-and-run attacks, or guerrilla raids, against Israeli settlements near the borders of other nations. Egypt recruited guerrillas, armed them, provided them with basic training, and paid them. Similar units formed inside the Jordanian-held West Bank and within the ranks of the Syrian army.

Bordering Israel, Egypt produced the first Palestinian terrorist groups.

| **FATAH** | One of the first important fedayeen movements to emerge was Harakat al-Tahrir al-Watani al-Filastini (Palestinian National Liberation Movement), better known as Fatah. Born out of a student

movement in Cairo, Egypt, in the 1950s, Fatah was founded by the Palestinians Yasser Arafat and Khalil Wazir. The group evolved from a loose political organization into an armed militia (military-like force). Members set up camps on the West Bank, in the Gaza Strip, and in the Syrian-controlled Golan Heights area. With more than two thousand men and women in arms, Fatah soon became the main power inside the

YASSER ARAFAT

Perhaps no single person represents the unfulfilled dream of the Palestinian people—or the unchecked horrors of indiscriminate violence—as powerfully as Yasser Arafat. Mohammed Abdel Rahman Abdel Raouf Arafat al-Qudwa al-Husseini (Arafat's given name) was born in Cairo on August 24, 1929, to Palestinian parents working in the Egyptian capital. In 1948 Arafat joined the fight against the fledgling Jewish state. Afterward, he returned to Egypt, where he began to organize and lead Palestinian student activists. By the late 1950s, he had founded Fatah and had set up a base

Yasser Arafat wearing the kaffiyeh

of operations on the West Bank, from which armed guerrillas launched terrorist attacks against border settlements in Israel.

Distinctive in his kaffiyeh (a black-and-white headdress), Arafat soon became the most prominent leader and symbol of the Palestinians. His image was enhanced by his uncanny ability to stay one step ahead of pursuing Israeli forces and of the assassin's bullet. Arafat always seemed to find a way to escape and survive to fight another day.

But, with Fatah involved in terrorism, Arafat also became the face of international terrorism.

Arafat has pursued a tireless political campaign to solidify international support for a Palestinian state. At the same time, he is believed by many to command Palestinian terrorist operations around the world. This double role has made Arafat one of the most controversial figures of the Arab-Israeli conflict. ■

A bomb planted by Fatah fedayeen overturned this truck carrying food to an Israeli market.

Palestine Liberation Organization (PLO). This umbrella group was founded in 1964 to represent all of the Palestinian revolutionary and armed liberation movements. Most of Fatah's early attacks were restricted to hit-and-run attacks against Israeli border towns and against resources such as water-supply facilities. The Israelis viewed the Palestinian raiders as terrorists. Palestinians viewed their guerrillas as freedom fighters.

■■■■■■■■■■■■■■■■■■■■■■■■■■■■

A Fatah Raid

The Fatah fedayeen *moved slowly that frigid night—January 1, 1965. Winter rains had made the hills a muddy mess, and the men found the five-mile march hard work. Dressed in lizard-pattern camouflage fatigues and the trademark kaffiyeh wrapped around their faces, the fedayeen moved sluggishly across the slippery hills, careful not to set off any trip wires or alert Israeli patrols. Their mission this cold winter's night was to destroy a water pipeline that supplied an arid nation with precious drinking and agricultural water. The operation would put Fatah on the map and signal the first shot in Palestine's war for liberation.*

It took hours for the fedayeen squad to reach the sound of flowing water by the Sea of Galilee. In the dark, each man shrugged off his canvas pack and removed the explosive charges inside. In the Syrian camps where they had trained for months, the squad members had learned how to assemble explosive devices quickly— even blindfolded. Inside Israel, though, the squad fumbled. Hands trembled from the cold and from fear, but no one spoke. Next to the water pipeline, leading from the juncture of sea and river, one man dug a small hole with the wooden gunstock of his Soviet-built AK-47 assault rifle. The charges were dropped into the hole, the timer initiated, and the spot covered with branches and twigs. The device was set to explode just before 5:00 A.M., one hour before the Israeli sentries would give the area one last look before daybreak. When the bombs went off, the terrorists hoped, Israel's national pipeline would lie in ruins. A faulty bomb foiled the plan, but the setback would not be enough to diminish Fatah's determination.

■ ■

| WAR RETURNS | By June 1967, regional tensions in the Middle East had been rising steadily for months. Fatah attacks from the Gaza Strip, the West Bank, and the Golan Heights had escalated, sparking Israeli hostility. Meanwhile, hundreds of thousands of Palestinians still languished in refugee camps. As the friction mounted, the region

Jordanian tanks threaten the Israeli border
just before the Six-Day War.

prepared for war. Egyptian troops crossed the Suez Canal into the Sinai Peninsula and advanced toward Israel. The Syrian and Jordanian armies also geared up for battle. With hostile enemies closing in, Israel launched an unexpected preemptive strike.

■ ■

The 1967 War

June 5, 1967, 5:00 A.M.: The sun had not yet risen over the eastern Judaean Hills, but the Israeli pilots couldn't sleep. They were too nervous. Sitting in briefing rooms in air bases throughout Israel, the pilots—many of them youths recently graduated from training—waited to receive their orders and targets.

The Israeli pilots knew that they would have to kill or be killed that morning. But the fight for their homeland was worth the risks. Some of them were tenth-generation Israelis whose parents had lived in the land under Turkish and British rule. Others were children of Holocaust survivors. With war looming, the pilots knew that the best chance the Israel Defense Forces had of facing the numerical superiority of the Arab armies was an all-out preemptive strike. Modern warfare depended on aerial prowess. If Israel were going to fight the combined Arab forces, Arab airpower had to be completely obliterated. Surprise—and a crippling first blow—were key to the day's daring mission. Just after dawn, the combat aircraft of the Israeli Air Force were fueled, loaded with ammunition and supplies, and dispatched toward more than thirty air force bases in Egypt, Syria, Jordan, and Iraq.

7:45 A.M.: In the officer's mess hall at the Heliopolis Air Force Base near Cairo, it was breakfast time. The pilots of the MiG-21 squadron had just finished their morning patrols. Egypt was readying itself for war, but the skies over the pyramids were clear of enemy activity that sunny June morning. The pilots talked and joked as they relaxed, drank sweet mint tea, and ate hummus, salad, and fried eggs in spicy tomato sauce. Ground crews tended to the aircraft after the morning flights.

Suddenly, explosions rattled the base's windows. Israeli aircraft—flying low to avoid radar detection—swept in and attacked in neat, precise formations, leaving huge craters in the

runways and pummeling MiG and Sukhoi fighters with 30mm cannon fire. By the time the Arab pilots ran for their planes, the aircraft were already smoldering ruins on the sun-baked runways. The Israeli Air Force had destroyed more than three hundred Arab aircraft. The 1967 War—also known as the Six-Day War—had begun.

Moments into the 1967 War, Egyptian planes lay demolished on air base runways throughout the country.

■ ■

Without air cover, the Arab armies were no match for Israeli forces. In just six days of bitter combat, the Israeli military captured the Sinai and the Gaza Strip from Egypt, the West Bank from Jordan, and the Golan Heights from Syria.

Once again, Palestinians living in the newly captured areas fled. Thousands of refugees flooded across the shallow Jordan River into Jordan. A deep hopelessness among Palestinians was intensified by the Arab world's military humiliation at this second Israeli military victory in a generation. It was not eased by UN Resolution 242. Passed unanimously by the United Nations, the resolution returned some of the territory captured by Israel to the Arab nations. However, it failed to mention explicitly the situation of displaced Palestinians. Feeling abandoned by the international community, many Palestinians felt that it was time to take the liberation movement to a new level. Meanwhile, Arafat and his Fatah guerrillas set up a base of operations in Jordan and prepared for strikes against Israeli towns and military outposts. Fatah operations were bloody, and Israel responded to each attack with retaliatory strikes against Palestinian targets in Jordan. The conflict intensified.

RAISING THE STAKES:

THE POPULAR FRONT FOR THE LIBERATION OF PALESTINE

T o most Palestinians, Fatah's strikes, while dramatic, accomplished little. The frustration created by this lack of progress led to the creation of many new organizations dedicated to expanding the struggle. These groups were prepared to take the fight for a Palestinian state to new levels of violence.

One of the most influential movements to emerge was the

George Habash, founder of the PFLP

Popular Front for the Liberation of Palestine (PFLP). The PFLP was founded in 1967 by George Habash, a Greek Orthodox Christian doctor. Originally from Lydda (once part of British Palestine and later of Lod, Israel), Habash was rumored to hand out PFLP ideas along with prescriptions in the Palestinian refugee clinic that he had founded in Amman, Jordan. The PFLP's objective was to create a Palestinian homeland built on the idea of Communism, a political and economic system based on the idea of common, rather than private, property, and the equal distribution of that property. With this goal in mind, Habash recruited working-class Palestinians who wanted a homeland that would be both politically independent and economically progressive.

A NEW FORM OF TERROR

The PFLP viewed terrorism as a legitimate tool with which to achieve statehood, regardless of the consequences to innocent life. Spearheading the PFLP terrorist campaign was Wadi Haddad, another Greek Orthodox doctor, who was known in Palestinian circles as the "Mastermind." Haddad and other PFLP leaders surmised that to publicize the Palestinian cause, as well as to attack Israel, they would have to strike at a target that would get international attention.

■ ■

Terror in the Skies

The mood at Rome's airport *on the night of July 23, 1968, was festive. Passengers on El Al Israel Airlines Flight 423, with nonstop service from Rome, Italy, to Tel Aviv, Israel, were boarding the plane. Many were returning from vacations in Italy, where they had been able to enjoy the sights and to escape, for a few days, the dangers of life in Israel. Airport security wasn't tight. Terrorism was something that happened in border towns in Jordan, not in the Italian capital.*

Three men stood quietly together in the passenger line. Hidden inside their specially made camera bags were pistols and grenades. Once on board the plane, they listened politely as the flight attendants presented safety tips prior to takeoff. But when the aircraft reached its cruising altitude of 25,000 feet, the three men unbuckled their seat belts, removed their weapons, and burst through the cockpit door. Threatening to blow up the aircraft unless their every instruction were followed to the letter, the hijackers ordered the pilot to divert the jet to Algiers, Algeria. The passengers were told to remain quiet and to stay in their seats. Anyone who resisted would be shot in the face.

What began as a two-hour flight turned into a weeks-long ordeal. The Algerian government, sympathetic to the Palestinian cause, held Israeli passengers for forty days while the negotiations for their release took place between the Israeli government and the terrorists. Concluding that they had no viable military way to rescue the

The hijacked El Al jet finally returned to Israel on
September 1, after more than a month of terror.

*captives, Israeli leaders finally agreed to the terrorists' demand and
released Palestinian prisoners from Israeli jails. Protected by
supportive Algerian officials, the hijackers themselves were not caught.*

■■■■■■■■■■■■■■■■■■■■■■■■■■■■■■■■

PFLP leaders felt a rush of victory after the El Al hijacking. Their
attack had not only terrorized the international public, it had forced the
Israeli government to give in to terrorism. PFLP planners were not willing
to rest. They intended to up the ante of violence, with another dramatic
display of terror that the whole world would see.

■■■■■■■■■■■■■■■■■■■■■■■■■■■■■■■■

Skyjack Sunday

On Sunday, September 6, 1970, *air travelers in Frankfurt,
a city in what was then West Germany, in Zürich, Switzerland, and
in Amsterdam, the Netherlands, were going about their business as
usual. They had no idea that a massive and coordinated terrorist
attack was about to change their lives forever.*

*On the day that came to be known as Skyjack Sunday, PFLP
operatives pulled off one swift, orchestrated operation that left the
international community stunned. The terrorists hijacked a TWA*

flight from Frankfurt, a Swissair flight from Zürich, a Pan Am flight from Amsterdam, and an El Al flight from Amsterdam. El Al security guards—determined to avoid a repeat of the Flight 423 hijacking—foiled the attack on their aircraft, killing one terrorist and capturing the other. That plane landed safely in London, England. Meanwhile, the hijackers on the TWA and Swissair flights diverted those planes to Dawson's Field, a remote strip of land in the desert near Amman, Jordan. The Pan Am plane—a Boeing 747 too large to land in Dawson's Field—was hijacked to Cairo.

A few days later, while the captive passengers on the three planes trembled in fear, PFLP operatives avenged the foiling of the El Al hijacking by hijacking a British flight and landing it at Dawson's Field. The drama at the airfield lasted nearly a week and captured the attention of the world, as international news reporters converged on the site. Finally, the terrorists ordered the hostages to deplane the oven-like aircraft at Dawson's Field and in Cairo. Then, in an act that would symbolize the wrath of terrorism for years to come, they blew up the planes. No passengers were killed.

■ ■

| AFTERMATH | The audacious Skyjack Sunday operation dramatically demonstrated the PFLP's ability to strike at numerous targets in different locations in a single day, with few repercussions. The only terrorist to be caught had been aboard the El Al flight, and that terrorist, Leila Khaled, was released by British authorities after the fifth hijacking. But the use of Jordan as a base for international terrorist attacks outraged the nation's leader, King Hussein. On September 17, on Hussein's orders, Jordanian armed forces stormed the refugee camps in and around Amman with the aim of crushing any groups of Palestinian guerrillas that were operating from those camps.

Syria then invaded Jordan in support of the Palestinians, prompting Israel to promise Jordan military aid. The conflict that followed was bloody. Thousands of Palestinian fighters and civilians were killed. Arafat's Fatah, the PFLP, and the other Palestinian resistance movements were forced to flee Jordan and head north to Syria and then to Lebanon, where they would set up new bases of operations against Israel.

LEILA KHALED

Palestinian groups have employed many women in the struggle against the Jewish state. The most famous female Palestinian terrorist was Leila Khaled, who became an international celebrity for her deeds.

Khaled was born in Haifa in 1944. Moving with her family to Lebanon after the 1948 War, the young Leila observed the misery of Palestinian refugees. She joined the PFLP shortly after it was formed and promptly underwent intensive training for operations against Israel.

Khaled's first assignment came on August 29, 1969. She and a PFLP comrade boarded a TWA jet flying from Rome to Athens, Greece. Brandishing guns and hand grenades, they hijacked the plane and diverted it to Damascus, Syria, where Khaled and her partner released their captives before destroying the plane. Although the two terrorists were held briefly in Syria, Syrian authorities—who were either sympathetic or frightened of becoming targets—soon released them to rejoin their PFLP comrades.

Before executing another major attack, Khaled underwent plastic surgery to disguise her features, which, after the 1969 hijacking, had become recognizable around the world. Then, on September 6, 1970, Khaled and a PFLP comrade took part in Skyjack Sunday. Their mission was to take over the El Al jet. However, when onboard, El Al security officials intervened, Khaled's partner was killed, and she was captured. The aircraft made an emergency landing in London, where Khaled was handed over to British authorities. Three days later, the PFLP hijacked the fifth jet of the Skyjack Sunday operation—a British airliner that the terrorists flew to Jordan. In exchange for the safe return of the plane's passengers, British authorities released Khaled.

Khaled retired from her short but notorious career in terrorism following Skyjack Sunday. Dedicated to the Palestinian cause, she still speaks out for a Palestinian homeland. ∎

PALESTINE

FIGHTERS
GENERATION AFTER GENERATION
UNTIL TOTAL LIBERATION

This poster, advocating a free Palestine, shows Leila Khaled in the Palestinian kaffiyeh.

Black September

Jordanian paratroopers crouched in Amman's narrow alleys, deafened by the incessant barrage of machine-gun fire from the alley's cramped houses. The neighborhood was a Palestinian stronghold, and the fedayeen were deeply entrenched. Explosive charges, ready to be detonated, ringed the streets. Machine-gun nests lined the rooftops. The fighters brandished weapons ranging from stones and bare fists to bayonets and firearms. King Hussein had summoned the Royal Jordanian Air Force's elite F-104 Starfighters to support the beleaguered troops pressing themselves against bullet-scarred stone walls. High-tech Centurion tanks were also on hand to support the Jordanians, ready to fire 105mm rounds into the homes from which the Palestinians were shooting.

The Palestinians, many of whom were refugees and not terrorist operatives, were courageous—and cruel—fighters. Captured Jordanian soldiers were tortured, then executed with bullets to the head. The Jordanian troops took no prisoners either. Seized fedayeen were tied to the backs of armored cars and dragged through the streets until all that remained were tatters of cloth and flesh.

Heavily armed Palestinians fight Jordanian troops in Amman in September 1970.

That infamous month of September 1970 was seen by Palestinians as one of the darkest periods in the history of their people. It became known as Aylul al-Aswad: Black September.

THE
VENGEANCE
OF
BLACK SEPTEMBER

To avenge the violence of Black September, Fatah commanders created a violent and radical new terrorist force. Called the Black September Organization, the group was conceived in September 1971. Referred to as a "deniable" special operations force, the group would appear to act independently (so the PLO could deny responsibility) but would actually work in the interests of the PLO and Fatah. Black September's objective was to commit large-scale and high-profile operations throughout the world against Jordanian and Israeli targets. The group's leaders were young, ambitious, and eager to prove their worth.

BLOODY BEGINNINGS

Black September's first major attack was the assassination of Jordan's prime minister, Wasfi Tal, who was fatally shot as he walked out of Cairo's Sheraton Hotel on November 28, 1971. The group went on to attempt assassinations of other Jordanian politicians and to attack Jordanian and Israeli targets around the world.

Another significant attack came on May 8, 1972, when four Black September terrorists hijacked a Sabena Belgian Airlines jet flying from Brussels, Belgium, to Israel. On the ground in Israel, the hijackers demanded the release of more than three hundred Palestinian operatives being held in Israeli jails. If the prisoners were not released, the terrorists threatened, the hostages aboard the plane would be executed.

But the plot was foiled when a group of elite Israeli commandos, led by future Israeli prime minister Ehud Barak, stormed the aircraft in a daring rescue mission. In the terrifying and chaotic minutes that followed, two of the Black September terrorists were killed, the other two were

Hostages are helped off the Sabena aircraft after Black September's hijacking operation was foiled by Israeli commandos.

captured, and one passenger was killed. However, all of the remaining captives were saved and were helped—shaken but safe—off of the plane.

The dramatic Sabena hijacking and rescue received a great deal of attention in the Israeli press. But it was not until September 1972, during the Summer Olympic Games in Munich, West Germany, that the full extent of the Palestinian terrorist offensive was broadcast to a truly global audience.

■ ■

The Munich Olympic Massacre

At 4:30 A.M. on September 5, 1972, *eight Black September terrorists, dressed as athletes and carrying their weapons in gym bags, stormed the living quarters of the Israeli Olympic team. They burst through the door, killing two of the team members and taking nine others hostage. The terrorists demanded the release of two hundred Palestinian terrorists jailed in Israel as well as safe passage out of West Germany for themselves and the Israeli hostages. With about one hundred television networks covering the 1972 Summer Olympics, the Black September attack became a "via satellite" drama. The image of the armed and hooded terrorists, standing on the balcony of the Israelis' quarters as they kept a watchful eye on West*

German police, would be seared onto the world's memory as a symbol of terrorism's rage and brutality.

For the entire day, as cameras rolled, West German officials tried to negotiate with the terrorists to secure the release of the Israeli captives. Israeli prime minister Golda Meir refused to make a deal with the terrorists, but she offered to send Israeli commandos into West Germany to storm the compound and end the ordeal. However, West Germany had hoped that the Olympics—dubbed the games of peace— would erase memories of the country's Nazi past. West German officials were eager to rescue the Jewish hostages by themselves.

It was to prove a tragic error in judgment. West German negotiators agreed to provide the Black September operatives with a jet to fly them and their captives out of the country. West German police then planned to ambush the terrorists at the nearby Fürstenfeldbruck airfield late on the night of September 5. The terrorists and their hostages were flown to the airfield in two helicopters, arriving at the tarmac where the snipers waited. But the ambush failed. The West German police were both too few in number and inadequately equipped for the task at hand. Only five snipers were in place, none of whom had extensive training or tools such as

A Black September terrorist looks out the window of the Israeli hostages' apartment during the Munich crisis.

walkie-talkies or night-vision rifle sights. A desperate battle between West German police snipers and the Black September terrorists followed. By the early hours of September 6, it was over. The snipers had killed five of the Palestinians. But before they had, the terrorists had killed one police officer and all nine Israeli hostages, turning machine guns on them and tossing grenades into the helicopters where they were still trapped.

■ ■

The three surviving Black September terrorists were captured and held by West German authorities. But in October, Palestinian terrorists—believed to be Fatah members—hijacked a Lufthansa plane carrying German passengers and demanded the release of the Black September operatives. West German officials complied. The Lufthansa plane and passengers were released, and the hijackers were not arrested. Some observers suspected that the West Germans, afraid of being targeted by other Palestinian groups, had secretly made a deal with the Palestinians to stage the Lufthansa hijacking as an excuse for the Black September terrorists' release.

| A CHANGED WORLD |

Munich was a watershed event in many ways. More than one billion people had followed the grim drama on television, making it the first attack to introduce the reality of terrorism to a global audience. Even as it horrified most of the world, in the eyes of some militants the attack was a monumental success. A few days after the massacre, a PLO spokesperson told an Arabic-language newspaper that "a bomb in the White House . . . could not have echoed through the consciousnesses of every man in the world like the operation at Munich . . . it was like painting the name of Palestine on the top of a mountain that can be seen from the four corners of the earth." To Palestinian terrorist groups, Munich demonstrated an irrefutable truth: the more shocking and spectacular the operation, the more publicity the organization and its cause received.

Munich also changed the way nations fought terrorism. Immediately following the Munich Olympic Massacre, the West German police, along with police and military organizations around the world, created elite counterterrorist hostage-rescue units that could respond forcefully—and successfully—to any terrorist attack. For Israel, in particular, the massacre at Munich was a call to greater and more aggressive action. The murder of eleven defenseless athletes spurred Israeli leaders to dedicate the nation's military forces and intelligence services to an unrelenting war against Palestinian terrorist groups—especially against Black September. In the years that followed the Munich Olympic Massacre, agents of the Mossad, Israel's foreign intelligence service, carried out Operation Wrath of God. In this operation, ordered by Golda Meir, Mossad commandos and spies hunted down and assassinated the Black September terrorists responsible for the Munich attack.

Israeli prime minister Golda Meir

Black September members did carry out one operation after Munich. In March 1973, eight terrorists seized the Saudi Arabian embassy in Khartoum, Sudan. They assassinated two American diplomats and one Belgian official before being arrested. The group largely faded from the scene soon after that assault. However, its legacy of tragedy and terror—and its impact on international counterterrorism—live on.

Splintering:
The Rejectionists

Despite brutal operations such as those carried out by Black September, many people in the Palestinian liberation movements wanted to see still greater action. They continued to support terrorism as the most effective way to bring international attention to the Palestinian struggle. Some of the most extreme groups also rejected the idea of political settlement with the Jewish state. These "rejectionists," as they became known, believed that the war against Israel should not end until the Palestinian flag flew not only over Jerusalem, but over all of Israel. Any Palestinian leader who negotiated with Israel or sought peace risked being marked for assassination by the rejectionists.

One rejectionist group to emerge from these feelings was the Popular Front for the Liberation of Palestine General Command, or PFLP-GC. This group was partly made up of PFLP members who felt that the organization was neither radical enough in its philosophy nor militant enough in its fight against Israel. Founded in 1968, the PFLP-GC was commanded by Ahmed Jibril. Jibril's political philosophy was total war against Israel and its allies.

Supported by Syria and Iran, Jibril's group was a highly organized military-like force of approximately one thousand operatives determined to use innovative and high-tech methods in their attacks. For

PFLP-GC commander Ahmed Jibril

TECHNO-TERRORISM

Ahmed Jibril—founder and commander of the PFLP-GC—baffled Israeli counterterrorism forces. Jibril's methods of attack made him the modern world's first techno-terrorist.

Born in a Palestinian village in 1929, Jibril moved to Syria and joined the army there as a young man. He excelled as a soldier and as a commander. More important to his future career in terrorism was the valuable experience that he gained as a combat engineer.

In the early 1960s, Jibril assembled an armed Palestinian force to engage in guerrilla attacks against Israel. In 1967 the group merged with Dr. George Habash's Popular Front for the Liberation of Palestine. But political and ideological differences soon led Jibril to split from the organization to form the PFLP-GC.

Built along military lines, the PFLP-GC was divided into platoons and squads like an army. Military discipline was the rule. But the group's unusual methods were what set it apart as a new kind of threat. Jibril himself designed and built remote-controlled rocket launchers that his operatives used to strike Israeli civilian targets along the Lebanese border. He also designed an altimeter bomb that, if placed on board before takeoff, was capable of bringing down an airliner flying at 30,000 feet. Jibril also used hang gliders, hot-air balloons, and racing boats to move operatives into Israel. These innovative tactics brought Jibril and his group notoriety as a major threat to Israel. ∎

example, on February 21, 1970, the PFLP-GC used altimeter bombs (explosive devices designed to explode when air pressure reaches a preset level) to destroy a Swissair jet en route to Israel as it flew over the Alps. The blast killed the forty-seven passengers and crewmembers on board. Investigators were not certain how the group had planted the bombs, but the explosives may have been in checked luggage.

| THE YOM KIPPUR WAR | On October 6, 1973—on Yom Kippur, the most important holiday on the Jewish calendar—the Egyptian and Syrian armies launched a massive surprise attack against Israel. Egyptian soldiers streamed across the Suez Canal onto the Sinai Peninsula. Syrian infantry pushed into the Golan Heights, threatening to charge all the way into northern Israel. In just over two weeks of brutal combat, the Israel Defense Forces (IDF) managed not only to stem the tide of the

Arab advance but to counterattack with considerable force. By the time a cease-fire was reached on October 22, 1973, Israeli tanks were only one hundred miles from Cairo and thirty miles from Damascus.

The 1973 War, sometimes called the Yom Kippur War, was a wake-up call for many Middle Eastern leaders. At first, the scope of the surprise attack had raised hopes in Arab nations that they could finally defeat Israel militarily. But the outcome—another military loss for the Arab powers—seemed proof that only diplomacy and compromise could end the Arab-Israeli dispute.

Many Palestinians wanted an end to terror and sought peace through political action. Through their efforts, the Palestinians had made some major diplomatic strides. They had gained a measure of international support for the establishment of a homeland as well as political acceptance of the PLO as the sole representative of the Palestinian people. The success of this Palestinian campaign reached its peak in 1974, when

Soldiers raise the Israeli flag on Mount Hermon in the Golan Heights during the 1973 War. The peak is one of the region's highest points.

PLO chairman Yasser Arafat was invited to address the General Assembly of the United Nations.

| GROWING FORCE | Yet rejectionist groups still hated the thought of compromise, and new groups arose to further the struggle. One rejectionist group that launched large-scale attacks against Israel was Nayef Hawatmeh's Democratic Front for the Liberation of Palestine, or DFLP. The DFLP arose at about the same time as the PFLP-GC, when Hawatmeh, one of George Habash's top commanders, left the PFLP to form a Communist-oriented military movement. Hawatmeh focused his military goals on spectacular attacks against targets inside Israel.

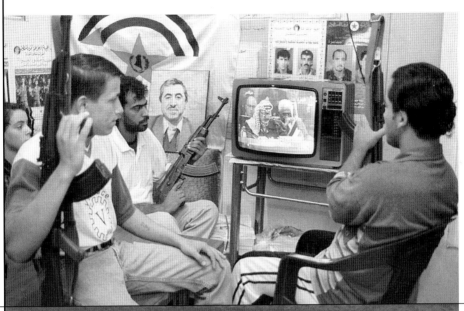

DFLP members meet in Beirut. The portrait *(back left)* is of the group's leader Nayef Hawatmeh.

■ ■

The Maalot Massacre

May 15, 1974, would go down in Israeli history as a day of sorrow and anger. Disguised as Israeli soldiers and armed with hand grenades and rifles, three DFLP gunmen crossed the Lebanese border into Israel. They attacked the Maalot schoolhouse, taking more than one hundred students as hostages and demanding that Israel release scores of Palestinian prisoners.

The Israeli commandos who gathered near the school knew that this rescue operation would be a grueling challenge. They were trained to venture deep behind enemy lines to carry out daring missions. They were also trained in hostage rescue and were skilled at storming planes, buses, or buildings where terrorists held captives at gunpoint. But here the odds were different. The hostages were schoolchildren.

Northern Israel was often targeted by terrorists.

The men holding them were prepared to die. As the commandos readied their gear, the mothers, fathers, brothers, and sisters of the hostages waited anxiously beyond the police barricades. Their fear filled the air.

The commandos were charged with ending the ordeal with a swift and unforgiving assault. They knew that the terrorists in the schoolhouse were no match for their skill and weapons proficiency. But they feared that the terrorists would turn their weapons on the

An Israeli commando helps one of the Maalot attack's victims out of the building, while other troops head inside.

children—and their fears were justified. Before the three terrorists were killed, they were able to carry out a horrific bloodbath. Bloodied by gunfire and burned from grenade explosions, some of the children leaped out of windows, screaming for their parents. Parents, breaking through the barriers, rushed into the school to search frantically for their children amid the smoke. The village began burying nearly two dozen children the next day, and Israel once again found itself in mourning.

■ ■

As PFLP offshoots formed and the Palestinian movement grew still broader, more outside nations played roles in the conflict. Communist China, North Korea, and the Soviet Union supported the DFLP, and many Arab states offered their assistance to other groups. The PFLP itself also cooperated with foreign groups to launch complex operations. One of the most famous such collaborations took place on June 27, 1976, when operatives from the PFLP and the Baader-Meinhof Gang, a German terrorist group, hijacked an Air France plane flying from Greece to Israel. The terrorists redirected the flight to Entebbe, Uganda, where Ugandan officials also cooperated with the attack. The operatives freed all but their Jewish hostages, demanding the release of Palestinian and German prisoners. After a weeklong standoff, IDF commandos stormed the plane in a daring rescue. Two hostages and all of the terrorists were killed in the operation.

Meanwhile, still hoping to avenge their historic wartime losses, Arab states including Syria, Libya, and Iraq created and trained their own Palestinian rejectionist movements. These well-funded terrorist groups continued the war against Israel, as well as against Palestinians who supported compromise with Israel. One of the most prominent of these groups, especially after the 1973 War, was the Iraq-sponsored Arab Liberation Front, or ALF. Led by Abdul Rahim Ahmed, the group carried out numerous attacks against Israel from a base in Lebanon.

■ ■

Misgav Am

The border separating Israel from Lebanon *was a dangerous frontier area known as Bandit Country. Thick rows of barbed wire provided a clear and distinctive reminder of the dangers that lurked north of the fence. Still, life went on. People who lived in the northern agricultural settlements worked the fields, traveled to jobs in Haifa or Galilee, and raised families.*

Late on the night of April 6, 1980, five terrorists belonging to the Iraq-based Arab Liberation Front crossed the Lebanese border. The target of the raid was the agricultural settlement of Misgav Am and its nursery, where two dozen children

The Misgav Am massacre was one of the ALF's most vicious attacks.

were sleeping that chilly spring night. The ALF operatives attacked the nursery to hold the children hostage and to force Israel to free imprisoned Palestinian comrades. When Israeli commandos stormed the nursery amid the screams of terrified children, bullets began to fly. When it was over, one child, one Israeli soldier, and one adult civilian had been killed, along with all five terrorists.

■ ■

| **A NEW RUTHLESSNESS** | One of the largest and most violent of all the rejectionist groups was the Abu Nidal Organization. Founded by Abu Nidal—the nom de guerre (battle name) of Sabri al-Banna, a Palestinian native of Jaffa, Israel—the group carried out widespread attacks in the Middle East, Asia, South America, and Europe. Their operations included strikes against Palestinian militants considered to be too moderate. Abu Nidal's operatives were highly secretive, operating in isolated cells (subgroups) based in Libya, Syria, Sudan, Yemen, and Iraq. The group's underground nature was further protected by its use of several different names, including Fatah-RC, the Arab Revolutionary Brigades, and Black June.

Abu Nidal, whose battle name in Arabic means "father of the struggle."

The Abu Nidal Organization came to represent terrorism's unrestrained brutality. The terrorists recruited by the group were willing to die for their cause. The more sensational an operation, they believed, the greater the world's fear of the movement and its violence.

Abu Nidal operatives carried out dozens of attacks in twenty different countries. Yet one of its most infamous operations wasn't measured by its body count, but rather by its effect on politics in the region.

■ ■

Attack on an Ambassador
Shlomo Argov, Israel's ambassador to Great Britain, had just enjoyed a pleasant evening at London's Dorchester Hotel on June 3, 1982. He had joined eighty other ambassadors at a private

diplomatic affair in one of the British capital's fanciest hotels to eat, drink, talk politics, and discuss their nations' goals. Educated at Georgetown University, in Washington, D.C., Argov was a vibrant and eloquent representative of the Jewish state. The talk at the dinner had been of a fragile peace—and of the danger of another incident igniting the Middle East.

After dinner, as Argov walked through the dark to his car, an Abu Nidal operative silently approached. At point-blank range, he fired his automatic weapon into the ambassador's head. One of Argov's bodyguards returned fire, injuring the assailant, and two other Palestinians ran from the scene. The ambassador, seriously wounded, was rushed to a hospital. A trauma team saved Argov's life—but he was permanently paralyzed by the bullet lodged in his brain.

■ ■

Argov's attempted murder, combined with other terrorist activity and regional tensions, spurred the State of Israel to action. Determined to stop Palestinian terrorism, Israel launched military strikes against PLO bases in southern Lebanon—bases from which the PLO itself had also been launching terrorist strikes against Israel.

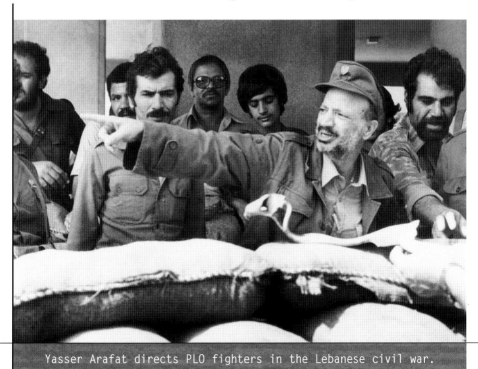

Yasser Arafat directs PLO fighters in the Lebanese civil war.

A full-scale Israeli invasion of Lebanon, which was already in the grip of a desperate civil war, began on June 6, 1982.

For Palestinian refugees living in Lebanon, the invasion and subsequent fighting were devastating. But the clashes did nothing to slow the tide of terrorism. In fact, the war left many Palestinian groups, including the Abu Nidal Organization, even more committed to the fight against Israel.

| **LAND AND SEA** | Another prominent rejectionist group was the Jabhat al-Tahrir al-Filistiniyyah, or Palestine Liberation Front (PLF). Muhammad Abbas, better known as Abu Abbas, was a former member of the PFLP-GC. He had split from the group to found the PLF, which was financially and politically supported by Libya and Iraq. The PLF's aim was to launch large-scale and innovative attacks against Israeli targets around the world.

The PLF attempted to cross the Israeli border from Lebanon several times, using both hang gliders and hot-air balloons. But seaborne attacks were the PLF's specialty.

PLF commander Abu Abbas

■ ■

Attack on the Achille Lauro
The four men kept to themselves inside their berth on the cruise ship Achille Lauro, *telling anyone who asked that they were Norwegian students on vacation. The ship was a pleasure cruise that stopped at a host of Mediterranean ports. A stop in Israel interested most of the American Jews onboard, many of whom were senior citizens. The stop in Israel was also of great interest to the "Norwegians"—who were actually well-trained operatives of the PLF. Their mission was to attack the arrivals hall at the Israeli port of Ashdod and carry out a massacre.*

Carrying AK-47 assault rifles and grenades, the terrorists planned to kill hundreds. But they were still several days from Ashdod on the afternoon of October 7, 1985, when a steward accidentally interrupted the four as they cleaned their weapons in their cabin. The terrorists panicked. Brandishing their guns and threatening to blow up the ship, the heavily armed operatives seized the cruise liner and more than four hundred passengers.

The hostages were beaten and terrorized by the PLF operatives. They took a particular interest in a sixty-nine-year-old Jewish New Yorker named Leon Klinghoffer. As the wheelchair-bound man sat helpless, the PLF operatives beat him and then fired an AK-47 round into the back of his head. Laughing, they tossed his body into the Mediterranean. It was, they thought, a great victory for Palestine.

British, Italian, and American commandos prepared to board the seized ocean liner, which the terrorists had diverted to Alexandria, Egypt. The terrorists had nowhere to run. When the ship docked, the operatives turned themselves in to Egyptian authorities—who permitted them to leave in an Egyptian plane. U.S. fighter planes then forced the terrorists to land in Sicily, an island off

Freed hostages sail to shore from the *Achille Lauro*, docked off the Egyptian coast.

Italy's southern coast. Italian authorities imprisoned the four seajackers, eventually trying and convicting them. But Abu Abbas, the mastermind of the operation, would remain free and in command of the PLF for many more years.

■ ■

| **ONGOING TERROR** | Even as Israel struggled to cope with emerging new groups, Abu Nidal remained on the scene. It maintained a reputation as the most dangerous, active, and murderous Palestinian terror organization of the period. Attacks in the mid-1980s included the hijacking of an Egyptian plane to Malta; grenade and machine-gun attacks against two European airports; and a suicide attack on a synagogue in Istanbul.

At the same time, other rejectionist groups continued their assault on Israel and its allies. Although Israeli commandos attempted to assassinate PLFP-GC leader Jibril in December 1988, the operation was unsuccessful. The Israeli raiding force sent dogs strapped with explosive charges into the labyrinth of tunnels in Jibril's underground headquarters in Lebanon, but entrenched PFLP-GC guerrillas fought back with great effectiveness. Jibril hid inside one of his bunkers and emerged from the fighting unscathed. Two weeks later, in an operation that was widely believed to have been a revenge plot masterminded by Jibril and executed by PFLP-GC operatives, Pan Am Flight 103 flying from London to New York City blew up over Lockerbie, Scotland. All 259 passengers were killed, along with 11 Lockerbie residents. The intensity of these rejectionist groups' campaigns of terror changed the face of international terrorism forever.

HOLY WAR
IN THE HOLY LAND:
THE
ISLAMIC MOVEMENTS

As the bloodshed continued, with no independent Palestinian state in sight, many Palestinians felt a growing sense of despair and anger. Convinced that the existing liberation groups were getting nowhere, some members of the Palestinian community's Muslim majority began looking to Islamic fundamentalism for answers.

| SHIFTING | Islamic fundamentalist groups reject European and American influence, support the establishment of Islamic governments, and follow a very strict interpretation of the Quran. Such groups had already been active in the Middle East for decades. The Muslim Brotherhood, a militant Islamic group formed in Egypt in 1928, maintained a strong presence among Palestinians in the Gaza Strip. The brotherhood's influence grew after the 1948 War, when thousands of Palestinian refugees turned to the brotherhood for support.

Following the 1967 War, however, most Palestinian liberation movements were based on secular (nonreligious) political ideas. In fact, many members of the Palestinian resistance were Christians, and several factions were led by Greek Orthodox Christians.

The spark for an explosion of Islamic fundamentalism was the 1979 revolution in Iran that brought the Ayatollah Khomeini to power. Meanwhile, Egyptian prime minister Anwar el-Sadat had signed a peace accord with Israel. Many Palestinians saw Egypt, the strongest Arab military and political power, as giving in to Israel. Islamic fundamentalists proclaimed that no secular system could effectively deal with the Israeli problem. Only Islam, they said, held the key to Palestine's liberation.

During this period of Islamic revival, the number of mosques in the West Bank nearly doubled, and the number in the Gaza Strip more than tripled. Gaza's Islamic University opened its doors. Fundamentalist charities and mosques established schools, libraries, youth groups, and free health clinics in the refugee camps of the Gaza Strip and the West Bank. The fundamentalist movement gathered a great amount of support from these activities, which reached out to the poorest and and most powerless Palestinians. The movement began to threaten the secular PLO's control over the occupied territories.

Although the vast majority of Islamic fundamentalists do not support violence as a way to achieve their goals, some of the most extreme fundamentalist groups eventually came to embrace terrorism as a tactic. One of the early Islamic terrorist groups to emerge for the Palestinian cause was the Harakat al-Jihad al-Islami al-Filastini, known in English as the Palestinian Islamic Jihad, or PIJ. The Arabic word "jihad" means a holy struggle or war, and the PIJ was a militant movement based on the Sunni branch of Islam—the sect to which nearly all Palestinian

In the 1970s, many young Palestinian Muslims, such as these students in the Gaza Strip, joined the Islamic fundamentalist movement.

48

Fathi Shaqaqi, leader
of the PIJ

Muslims belong. However, it was also inspired Iran's Ayatollah Khomeini, who belonged to the stricter Shiite sect of Islam.

Led by Fathi Shaqaqi, a doctor from the Gaza Strip, the PIJ appeared in the Gaza Strip and the West Bank in about 1979. Some of its first members were Palestinian students who had studied in Egypt and who had been involved in Palestinian activism there. Egypt was home to several fundamentalist groups, including al-Jihad, which assassinated Anwar el-Sadat in 1981 in retaliation for his peacemaking with Israel. In fact, the outlines of the PIJ may have actually been drawn in Egypt. But by the 1980s, the group had begun launching guerrilla attacks against Israel from bases in the Gaza Strip.

■ ■

Holy War Begins
Gaza had always been a dangerous assignment *for Israeli forces. Poor, congested, and the base of operations for multiple terrorist agencies, it was often the scene of bloodshed.*

For years the IDF, the Israeli Border Guards, and the Israeli police had tried to maintain law and order in Gaza. They knew the city well. They knew which neighborhoods were controlled by Fatah, the PFLP, and the DFLP. They knew, too, that Islamic fundamentalist groups such as the PIJ were based in the city, although they had never been very active.

But the mood in Gaza was changing. Gaza's mosques had become the source of comfort and guidance for many frustrated and hopeless Palestinians. The mosques offered answers. The mosques promised a holy path.

On a warm August afternoon in 1987, Captain Ron Tal, commander of the Israeli military police in the Gaza Strip, stopped his car at a red light. The street was packed with motorists, truck

Israeli Border Guards on patrol

drivers, beggars, and small children selling newspapers, trinkets,
and soft drinks. Captain Tal never saw the man, dressed in white
robes, approach the car, raise his weapon, and fire. Without
warning, Captain Tal became one of the first fatalities of the PIJ's
holy war against the Jewish state.

■ ■

PIJ terrorism eventually led Israeli authorities to deport Shaqaqi
and other PIJ members from the Gaza Strip to Lebanon in the late
1980s. However, Shaqaqi sought aid from Iran and Syria to fund the PIJ's
ongoing pursuit of a Palestinian Islamic state. These funds helped him to
establish new bases in several Middle Eastern nations and to remain
active in the Gaza Strip.

THE EMERGENCE OF HAMAS | As the PIJ gathered
strength, other Islamic groups also emerged. One of the most prominent
was Hamas (the Arabic acronym for Harakat al-Muqawama al-Islamiya,
or Islamic Resistance Movement).

Founded in 1987 by Sheikh Ahmed Yassin, a blind and wheelchair-
bound Muslim cleric, Hamas was small but fiercely dedicated. In the tradition
of the Muslim Brotherhood, Sheikh Yassin built the group as an underground

movement that preached secrecy and loyalty. Yassin's followers set up individual cells that gathered intelligence and sought out weapons. Meanwhile, Yassin opened schools, clinics, and clubs throughout the Gaza Strip as alternatives to the institutions that were run and funded by Arafat's PLO.

During the intifada, a major Palestinian uprising that began in 1987, Hamas squads attacked Israeli targets in isolated shooting incidents, stabbings, and small-scale bombings. In August 1988, Hamas published the Islamic Covenant, which challenged the PLO's claim of being the sole legitimate representative of the Palestinian people. Meanwhile, Hamas continued to recruit operatives in mosques and youth clubs. It also quietly established a secretive military arm in the Gaza Strip and the West Bank. Called the al-Majahadoun al-Falestinioun (Palestinian Holy Fighters), the group attacked secular Palestinian factions, as well as Israeli targets.

As its attacks grew bolder and broader, the al-Majahadoun al-Falestinioun grew into what became known as the Izzedine al-Qassam Brigades in Gaza and the Abdullah Azzam Brigades in the West Bank. These military cells carried out the kidnappings and brutal murders of several Israeli soldiers. In February 1989, Hamas operatives kidnapped Avi Sasportas, a young soldier hitching a ride to his base in southern Israel.

Palestinians used whatever weapons they had during the intifada. These West Bank residents use slingshots to take aim at an Israeli helicopter.

THE INTIFADA

The intifada—which literally means the "shaking"—began in November 1987 with the dull hum of a motorized hang glider as it flew low over the Lebanese border. The PFLP-GC terrorist at the controls flew undetected through the darkened Lebanese sky into northern Israel. Across the border, he proceeded toward an army post near the town of Qiryat Shemona, where he shot and killed six Israeli soldiers before being shot down by IDF troopers.

For the first time, a Palestinian terrorist had openly attacked an army position instead of a civilian target. The news that one Palestinian armed with an AK-47 could kill six Israeli soldiers was hailed in Palestinian refugee camps. The reports seemed to prove that Israeli soldiers were not as invincible as they appeared. Inside the occupied territories of the Gaza Strip and the West Bank, they were vastly outnumbered.

Inspired by the audacious attack, Palestinian youths began to demonstrate in the streets of Gaza and the West Bank, throwing stones and hurling insults at IDF troops and Israeli Border Guards. A few days later, a traffic accident killed four young Palestinians. When rumors began to circulate that an Israeli had deliberately caused the accident, rage spread throughout the Palestinian community. At the youths' funerals, protests and stone throwing broke out. Israeli soldiers on patrol shot one protester fatally, and large-scale demonstrations erupted overnight. The violence was spontaneous and widespread. Anyone who could throw a rock or shout an insult joined in. Israel, a nation that had faced down Arab military might, was suddenly being challenged by old women and young boys. ■

Many young people, such as these high school students in Gaza, joined the intifada uprising.

He was beaten, tortured, and executed. Two months later, Ilan Saadon, another soldier, was also abducted and murdered. The Shin Bet (Israel's domestic counterintelligence unit) rounded up hundreds of Hamas operatives, including Sheikh Ahmed Yassin. But these men, who had sworn to liberate Jerusalem in a holy war, would not budge under interrogation.

Sheikh Ahmed Yassin in the custody of Israeli security forces

In December 1992, the Hamas kidnapping and murder of an Israeli policeman prompted a swift and forceful response from Israel. Israeli authorities rounded up more than four hundred Hamas members and deported them to Lebanon. The Palestinians set up a simple camp in a neutral zone in the mountainous wasteland of southern Lebanon. Contrary to Israeli intentions, international news images of the deportees—portrayed as living in flimsy canvas tents pitched on windswept hills—invoked widespread sympathy for the Palestinians.

What the reporters' cameras did not show were the camp's nighttime visitors. After dark, commanders from Lebanon's Hezbollah, a fundamentalist terrorist group, arrived. Hezbollah had been one of the first groups in the world to make wide use of suicide bombers—terrorists who detonated explosives strapped to their own bodies or drove vehicles loaded with bombs into buildings. They viewed dying for their holy cause as the noblest of deaths, and suicide bombers were respected for their devotion.

The Hezbollah commanders that visited the Hamas camp trained the group's members in this devastating form of attack. Soon Hamas was ready to use that training to unleash a lethal wave of suicide bombings.

| TURNING POINTS |

On September 13, 1993, a historic handshake took place between PLO chairman Yasser Arafat and Israeli prime minister Yitzhak Rabin. Sealing a peace deal known as the Oslo Accords, the handshake was a turning point in the ongoing war between the Palestinians and the Israelis. Long considered by the Israelis as a terrorist and someone with whom they would never negotiate, Arafat had become, it appeared, a partner in peace. Arafat also gained greater political power, setting up an independent government called the Palestinian Authority that was expected to eventually control an independent Palestine. But to some people on both sides of the conflict, the deal was the ultimate act of treason, and they vowed to end the peace process. Hamas pledged a jihad against both Israel and the Palestinian

Prime Minister Yitzhak Rabin *(left)* and Yasser Arafat *(right)* shake hands for the first time, as U.S. president Bill Clinton *(center)* looks on.

Authority in the Gaza Strip and the West Bank. Jewish extremists pledged violence, too, viewing the State of Israel as land given to them by God and never to be compromised.

Troops stream into Hebron's Ibrahim Mosque following Baruch Goldstein's attack on worshipers there.

Early on the morning of February 25, 1994, about seven hundred children and adults had gathered in the Ibrahim Mosque in the West Bank city of Hebron. Suddenly, Dr. Baruch Goldstein, an American-born Israeli physician who lived in a nearby settlement, entered the mosque and opened fire on the crowd of worshipers. Before he was attacked and killed by onlookers, Goldstein fatally shot nearly thirty men, woman, and children and wounded dozens more. Riots erupted throughout the West Bank and the Gaza Strip, and Hamas vowed revenge.

■ ■

A Terrible Weapon

On April 6, 1994, *people were milling around the school in Afula, Israel. The afternoon was warm and sunny, with a cool breeze blowing from the north. Classes were over for the day. Kids streamed out of the high school, thinking about dating, parties, and sports. Busy parents, worried about parking spots and schedules, arrived to pick up their children. Optimism was in the air. Seven months ago, Rabin* *and Arafat had shaken hands in front of millions of onlookers to seal the Oslo Accords. Perhaps peace was finally at hand.*

Hamas shattered hopes of peace that day. Taking vengeance for the Hebron massacre, a young Hamas member watched the school from behind the wheel of a car. His vehicle was packed with homemade explosives. The bomb was studded with nails and screws to guarantee the greatest destruction possible. When the bomber saw a bus full of students pulling away from the school, he struck, blowing up the bombs— and himself. Eight civilians were killed. Nearly fifty were seriously wounded. For the moment, Hamas had closed the book on peace.

■ ■

Hamas suicide bombings were soon widespread within Israel. The attacks were partly intended to discredit Yasser Arafat as a peacemaker. In the eyes of Hamas leaders, the bombings would prove to the world that Arafat did not direct the course of the peace process and that he would never put a stop to terrorism. Hamas also hoped that the bloody attacks would topple the government of Prime Minister Rabin by convincing the Israeli public that his peacemaking policies were causing death in the nation's streets. Rabin vowed not to allow terrorism to derail the peace accords. However, a few Jewish terrorist groups also remained active, and the prime minister was ultimately assassinated by a Jewish extremist on November 4, 1995. Meanwhile, attacks continued. Between April 1994 and September 1997, Hamas and PIJ suicide bombings had killed nearly one hundred Israelis and wounded nearly one thousand.

This Hamas poster urges operatives to continue the fight to destroy Israel. The Palestinian flag waves behind the armed fighter.

AFTER SHAQAQI

On the night of October 29, 1995, a somber group of political leaders, military commanders, and others stood quietly on the runway of a remote airfield in Damascus. As a plane landed, the full military honor guard standing by saluted.

The plane bore the body of Fathi Shaqaqi. Until a few days earlier, he had served as the commander of the PIJ. In the course of a few violent years, the group had killed dozens of Israelis in a series of horrific suicide bombings. Earlier that month, Shaqaqi had traveled to Malta from Libya using a forged Libyan passport and a pseudonym. On October 26, he had been gunned down in the Maltese capital of Valletta by an unidentified motorcyclist, a suspected agent of Mossad. A few days later, the PIJ formally named Shaqaqi's successor: thirty-eight-year-old Ramadan Abdullah Shallah.

Shallah was one of the founders of the PIJ. But U.S. counterintelligence agents found Shallah's rise to the PIJ leadership especially troubling. From 1991 until just before he succeeded Shaqaqi, Shallah had lived in the United States—not as a fugitive but as a well-regarded economics professor and Islamic leader at the University of South Florida in Tampa.

Ramadan Abdullah Shallah recites the Quran at Shaqaqi's funeral.

Shallah had been known in Tampa as a quiet man who supported peace and tolerance in the Middle East. He had helped to form and run several university groups that promoted religious freedom and political moderation. But when the facts were reviewed after Shallah took over the PIJ, it appeared that those same groups were actually involved in terrorism. Shallah had been coordinating PIJ attacks on Israel, it was believed, right from his university office in Tampa. ∎

DIPLOMACY AND DEATH:
THE CONFLICT CONTINUES

After years of exile to Lebanon, Tunisia, and elsewhere in the region, Arafat arrived in the Gaza Strip in the mid-1990s to serve as president of the Palestinian Authority—a promising step toward statehood. But as the suicide-bombing campaign took life after life, Arafat took no action to stop the violence. Arafat's double role—promising peace while at the same time allowing terror to continue—angered many observers and threatened the peace process.

| A FRAGILE PEACE | For six years, the Palestinian Authority ruled the Gaza Strip and most of the West Bank. In July 2000,

Arafat and Israeli prime minister Ehud Barak met for a peace conference. The talks were intended to hammer out the final details of an accord that would result in statehood for the Palestinian people and safety for the Israelis. But the conference ended without a deal and with threats of war. Once again, the region trembled on the edge of violence. Then, on September 28, 2000, Israeli politician Ariel Sharon made a public visit to

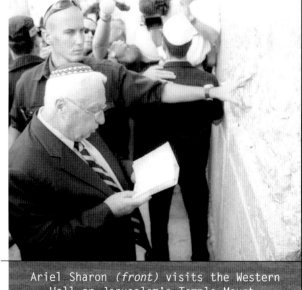

Ariel Sharon (front) visits the Western Wall on Jerusalem's Temple Mount.

Jerusalem's Temple Mount, an area that includes Jewish holy sites as well as the Dome of the Rock and the al-Aqsa Mosque. Sharon, standing near two of Islam's holiest sites, declared that Israel would never surrender Jerusalem to the Palestinians. Palestinians saw the act as highly provocative and rose up in the second intifada against Israel. The bloody struggle—which some observers believe was planned before Sharon's visit—became known as the al-Aqsa Intifada.

A surge in terrorist attacks soon followed. In December 2001, after several devastating suicide bombings in Jerusalem, Israeli military

Riots, bombings, and other violence increased dramatically in Israel and the disputed territories in 2000 and 2001.

forces bombed Arafat's headquarters in the Gaza Strip and destroyed the two helicopters he used to travel around the West Bank. The strikes drove Arafat to his West Bank headquarters, a compound named Muqata and located in the city of Ramallah.

| NEW THREATS | Even as the Israeli government took steps to weaken Arafat, Palestinian forces continued their attacks. One of the newest of these groups was a shadowy force known as the Tanzim.

THE COST OF THE AL-AQSA INTIFADA

The al-Aqsa Intifada has been one of the bloodiest conflicts fought between Arabs and Israelis. Hundreds of Israelis and Palestinians have been killed, and thousands have been wounded. Palestinian suicide bombings have marked the conflict. On June 1, 2001, a suicide bomber attacked a crowd of teenagers waiting to enter a Tel Aviv disco, killing twenty-one and wounding one hundred and twenty. On June 5, 2002, a car bombing near Afula killed seventeen and injured thirty-eight. On March 5, 2003, Hamas bombed a bus near Haifa's university, killing sixteen and wounding more than one hundred. Most Israeli casualties have been innocent civilians, and most have been males in their teens and twenties.

Hundreds of Palestinian young men have also been killed and wounded in the fighting. Many of them were fighters themselves, and some were killed by rival groups. However, many innocent Palestinians have lost their lives. In addition, Israeli forces have demolished hundreds of Palestinian houses. Some of these homes were destroyed because they were built in the Gaza Strip or on the West Bank without permits, while Palestinians claim that others were destroyed as collective punishment for terrorism. At the same time, the Israeli and Palestinian economies have both been hit hard as the violence deters tourists from visiting the area.

It is difficult to measure the cost of the intifada. But by any yardstick, both the Israeli and the Palestinian sides have suffered enormous losses in this ongoing conflict. ■

The al-Aqsa Intifada has seen many Israelis killed in bloody suicide bombings.

Meanwhile, many Palestinian homes have been demolished.

This armed militia had been set up in 1995 by Arafat and his Fatah leaders and was strongly loyal to Arafat. The Tanzim was designed to prevent any challenges to Arafat's leadership from Hamas or the PIJ. It was also founded as yet another opposition force against Israel.

The Tanzim, however, soon developed a direction of its own. It acted not only against Israel but also against some of the other Palestinian forces, and it emerged as a rival to Arafat and Fatah. Tanzim members portrayed themselves as the real future of a Palestinian state. They encouraged young Palestinians, often poor and uneducated, to join the struggle. The group's commander, Marwan Barghouti, was a charismatic leader who considered himself a possible successor to Arafat. Barghouti's eventual arrest and imprisonment in Israel for his activities caused an outrage among many Palestinians, but he continued to voice his support of the Tanzim and the intifada from his prison cell.

Tanzim commander Marwan Barghouti

As the Tanzim became more independent, it also widened its influence. It was subdivided into small cells with branches in almost every neighborhood, village, city, refugee camp, and school on the West Bank and in the Gaza Strip. The popular, well-funded force posed a grave threat to both Israeli troops and civilians.

■ ■

The Tanzim Strikes

The family had waited for this day for months. A bat mitzvah, a Jewish girl's thirteenth birthday celebration, was an important rite of passage that a family traditionally celebrated with a large party. On the night of January 17, 2002, the Armon David banquet hall in the town of Hadera was packed with about 180 partygoers enjoying a five-course meal in honor of a young girl.

At 10:45 P.M., a Tanzim terrorist burst into the hall and began firing his M16 assault rifle into the crowd. Moments later, the terrorist *fled into the night. Outside, police units that had rushed to the scene cut him down in a hail of fire. But before he was killed, the terrorist had murdered six of the partygoers and wounded thirty more.*

■ ■

The Tanzim's strike in Hadera left Israelis stunned. On March 27, 2002, another brutal attack spurred Israel to new action. The evening marked the first night of Passover, an important Jewish holiday. As families gathered at the Park Hotel in Netanya for the traditional Passover dinner called the seder, a Hamas suicide bomber struck, killing more than twenty and wounding more than one hundred. Two days later, Israel launched a full-scale military assault against Palestinian terrorist targets throughout the West Bank. Arafat's compound in Ramallah was surrounded, and Israel reoccupied most of the West Bank.

| A WAR ON TERROR | Aiding Israel's assault on Arafat was

a surge in international efforts to stamp out terrorism throughout the world. Following the September 11, 2001, terrorist attacks against the United States, which were planned and carried out by members of the Islamic fundamentalist group al-Qaeda, the United States declared a far-reaching War on Terror. With international opinion more inflamed than ever against all forms of terrorism, many observers hoped that Arafat would finally give up terrorism as a way to establish a Palestinian state. The opposite happened, however. Arafat's Fatah commanders had created yet another terrorist force, the al-Aqsa Martyrs Brigades. This fundamentalist Islamic group would join Hamas and the PIJ in launching a flood of suicide-bombing attacks.

■ ■

An al-Aqsa Martyr

Ayat Akhras was a popular, *studious eighteen-year-old. She went to school, helped around the house, and liked music and pop culture. But from inside her refugee camp, in the old section of Bethlehem, her pop culture was Fatah and the struggle against the Jewish state. She believed in the struggle, and she believed in the sacrifice that Fatah and other groups urged each Palestinian to make in the holy war to liberate Jerusalem. Recruiters for the Al-Aqsa*

Palestinian girls and women protesting against Israel
wave a photo of al-Aqsa Martyrs Brigades suicide bomber
Ayat Akhras *(upper left)*.

*Martyrs Brigades had enlisted her for a special mission. Ayat Akhras
was going to be a martyr.*

*On March 29, 2002, Akhras walked down a Jerusalem street
crowded with shoppers. Around her slim waist was a belt loaded with
explosives, hidden by loose clothing. As she approached the entrance
of a supermarket, a security guard stopped her. A split second later,
Akhras blew herself up in a blinding flash. She killed the guard and
a seventeen-year-old Israeli girl and wounded some two dozen others.*

■ ■

Young Palestinians such as Ayat Akhras and many others continue
to wage a tragic and vicious terrorist war against Israeli civilians. Hamas,
the PIJ, and the al-Aqsa Martyrs Brigades all carry out intense attacks.
Suicide bombings fill the news, alongside stories of Palestinian civilians in
the occupied territories being killed and injured in Israeli counterterrorism
operations. Palestinians also face severe restrictions on employment and
travel, imposed by Israel in response to terrorism. As the conflict wears
on, Palestinians and Israelis alike wonder if the violence will ever end.

EPILOGUE*

The Arab-Israeli situation remains unresolved. Despite developments such as the death of terrorist Abu Nidal, who was found shot in an Iraq apartment in August 2002, the tide of terrorism has not yet been stemmed. Regional tensions were further heightened in March 2003 by a U.S.-led war against Iraq. Waging a global War on Terror, U.S. forces fought in Iraq partly over suspicions that Iraqi president Saddam Hussein aided terrorism. That claim was supported in April, when U.S. forces in Baghdad captured PLF leader Abu Abbas. Nevertheless, to many people in the Middle East, the war seemed to be another case of Israel's allies targeting the Arab world. Anti-U.S. sentiment surged in the region.

However, promising steps are also being taken. Since mid-2002, U.S. officials have been working with international leaders to draft a "road map" for peace in the Arab-Israeli conflict. One requirement for a deal was new Palestinian leadership, as both the Israeli and the U.S. governments deemed Arafat an obstacle to peace. In March 2003, the Palestinian government chose Mahmoud Abbas as prime minister. Abbas, also known as Abu Mazen, was a founding member of Fatah and a longtime figure in Palestinian government.

Peace talks among Abu Mazen, Israeli prime minister Ariel Sharon, and other regional leaders took place in the spring and summer of 2003, and many observers hoped that a lasting peace was finally near. Renewed suicide bombings by Hamas—which rejected the road map—and retaliatory actions by Israel initially threatened progress toward that peace. Meanwhile, even with diminished power, Arafat remained entrenched. However, in July 2003, Hamas and other terrorist groups agreed to a three-month cease-fire, and Fatah agreed to a six-month truce. Israel also took steps toward a Palestinian state by withdrawing troops and turning over the security of selected areas, including Bethlehem on the West Bank, to Palestinian forces. Yet peace remains fragile. For the time being, both sides of the conflict can only wait and hope for an end to the many years of terror. ∎

*Please note that the information contained in this book was current at the time of publication. To find sources for late-breaking news, please consult the websites listed on page 69.

TIMELINE

1700s B.C.E.   Abraham moves to Canaan.

1100s B.C.E.   The Philistines settle along Canaan's southern coast.

900s B.C.E.   The First Temple is built in Jerusalem.

63 B.C.E.   The Roman Empire conquers Israel.

C.E. 70   The Second Temple is destroyed.

CA. 610   Muhammad founds Islam.

691   The Dome of the Rock is built in Jerusalem.

1000s-1200s   The Crusades take place.

1300s-1400s   The Mamluks control Palestine and the surrounding area.

1516   The Ottoman Empire conquers the region of Palestine.

1896   Theodor Herzl's *Der Judenstaat* is published, spurring the spread of modern Zionism.

1914   World War I begins.

1917   The Balfour Declaration is written.

1918   World War I ends. Palestine comes under British control.

1936-1939   The Palestinian Arab Revolt takes place.

1939-1945   World War II takes place. Six million Jews are killed in the Nazis' death camps.

1948   The State of Israel is declared. The Arabs and Israelis fight one another in 1948 War.

1964   The Palestine Liberation Organization is founded.

1967   The Six-Day War takes place. UN Resolution 242 is passed. George Habash forms the Popular Front for the Liberation of Palestine (PFLP).

1968	Ahmed Jibril forms the Popular Front for the Liberation of Palestine General Command (PFLP-GC). Habash's PFLP executes its first hijacking operation.
1969	The Arab Liberation Front (ALF) and the Democratic Front for the Liberation of Palestine (DFLP) are formed.
1970	Skyjack Sunday takes place. Jordanian troops begin an assault on Palestinian refugee camps, an event that comes to be known as Black September.
1972	Black September terrorists execute the Munich Olympic Massacre.
1973	The Yom Kippur War takes place.
1974	DFLP operatives carry out the Maalot Massacre.
1976	PFLP and Baader-Meinhof operatives hijack an Air France plane to Entebbe, Uganda. IDF commandos storm the plane and rescue the hostages.
1979	An Islamic revolution in Iran brings the Shiite Ayatollah Khomeini to power.
CA. 1980	Fathi Shaqaqi forms the Palestinian Islamic Jihad (PIJ). ALF terrorists execute an attack on the Israeli border town of Misgav Am.
1982	An Abu Nidal terrorist attempts to assassinate Israeli ambassador Shlomo Argov. Civil war begins in Lebanon.
1985	PFLP members attack the Italian ship *Achille Lauro.*
1987	The first intifada begins. Sheikh Ahmed Yassin forms Hamas. A PIJ attacker kills Israeli police captain Ron Tal.
1988	Hamas publishes the Islamic Covenant.
1989	Hamas terrorists kidnap and murder Israeli soldiers.

1993   Yasser Arafat and Yitzhak Rabin sign the Oslo
        Peace Accords.

1994   Dr. Baruch Goldstein kills and wounds dozens of
        worshipers at the Ibrahim Mosque in Hebron.
        Hamas carries out its first major suicide
        bombings inside Israel.

1995   The Tanzim is formed.

2000   The al-Aqsa Intifada begins. The al-Aqsa
        Martyrs Brigades are formed.

2002   A Tanzim terrorist attacks a bat mitzvah
        celebration in Hadera. A Hamas suicide bomber
        strikes a Passover dinner in Netanya. The
        attack becomes known as the Passover Massacre.

2003   Mahmoud Abbas becomes the Palestinian prime
        minister, taking over some of Arafat's power.
        A U.S.-led coalition goes to war against Iraq.
        PLF leader Abu Abbas is captured in Baghdad.
        International leaders meet to discuss the
        "road map" for peace.

SELECTED BIBLIOGRAPHY

Alexander, Yonah. *Palestinian Religious Terrorism: Hamas and Islamic Jihad*. Ardsley, NY: Transnational Publishers, 2002.

Bar-Zohar, Michael, and Eitan Haber. *The Quest for the Red Prince*. New York: William Morrow and Company, Inc., 1983.

Bickerton, Ian J., and Carla L. Klausner. *A Concise History of the Arab-Israeli Conflict*. 4th ed. Upper Saddle River, NJ: Prentice Hall, 2002.

Black, Ian, and Benny Morris. *Israel's Secret Wars: The Untold History of Israeli Intelligence*. London: Hamish Hamilton, 1991.

Dallas, Roland. *King Hussein: Life on the Edge*. New York: Fromm, 1999.

Dupuy, Trevor N. *Elusive Victory: The Arab-Israeli Wars 1947–74*. New York: Harper and Row, 1978.

El-Edroos, Brigadier S. A. *The Hashemite Arab Army 1908–1979*. Amman, Jordan: The Publishing Committee, 1980.

Goren, Roberta. *The Soviet Union and Terrorism*. London: George Allen and Unwin, 1984.

Henderson, Harry. *Global Terrorism: The Complete Reference Guide*. New York: Facts on File, 2001.

Herzog, Chaim. *The Arab-Israeli Wars*. London: Arms and Armour Press, 1982.

Hirst, David. *The Gun and the Olive Branch*. London: Futura Publications Limited, 1977.

Katz, Samuel M. *The Hunt for the Engineer: How Israeli Agents Tracked the Hamas Master Bomber*. New York: Fromm, 1999.

———. *Israel Versus Jibril: The Thirty Year War against a Master Terrorist*. New York: Paragon House, 1993.

Merari, Ariel, and Shlomi Elad. *The International Dimension of Palestinian Terrorism*. Boulder, CO: Westview Press, 1986.

Mishal, Shaul, and Avraham Sela. *The Palestinian Hamas*. New York: Columbia University Press, 2000.

O'Ballance, Edgar. *Arab Guerilla Power 1967–1972*. London: Faber and Faber, 1974.

El-Rayyes, Riad, and Dunia Nahas. *Guerrillas for Palestine*. New York: St. Martins Press, 1976.

Schiff, Zeev, and Raphael Rothstein. *Fedayeen: Guerrillas against Israel*. New York: David McKay Company, Inc., 1972.

Seale, Patrick. *Abu Nidal: A Gun for Hire*. New York: Random House, 1992.

Wallach, Janet, and John Wallach. *Arafat: In the Eyes of the Beholder*. New York: Birch Lane Press, 1997.

FURTHER READING AND WEBSITES

Books

Corzine, Phyllis. *The Palestinian-Israeli Accord*. San Diego: Lucent Books, 1997.

Currie, Stephen. *Terrorists and Terrorist Groups*. San Diego: Lucent Books, 2002.

Fridell, Ron. *Terrorism: Political Violence at Home and Abroad*. Berkeley Heights, NJ: Enslow Publishers, 2001.

Goldstein, Margaret. *Israel in Pictures*. Minneapolis, MN: Lerner Publications Company, 2004.

Headlam, George. *Yasser Arafat*. Minneapolis, MN: Lerner Publications Company, 2004.

Marcovitz, Hal. *Terrorism*. Philadelphia: Chelsea House Publishers, 2001.

Taylor, Robert. *The History of Terrorism*. San Diego: Lucent Books, 2002.

Websites

BBC News World Edition
<http://news.bbc.co.uk/>
This site provides extensive coverage of international news, along with an in-depth look at the Palestinian-Israeli conflict.

The Center for Defense Information: Terrorism Project
<http://www.cdi.org/terrorism>
This site provides detailed articles on a variety of topics related to terrorism.

CNN.com
<http://www.cnn.com>
This news site is a source of breaking news on terrorism and other world events. It also offers a searchable archive of past articles.

The New York Times on the Web
<http://nytimes.com>
Access current *New York Times* articles on terrorism and terrorist groups at this site, or search the archive for older materials.

Terrorism Questions and Answers
<http://www.terrorismanswers.com>
This site, operated by the Markle Foundation (a nonprofit group that studies communications and media), presents a wealth of information through question-and-answer sheets on various aspects of terrorism.

The Terrorism Research Center
<http://www.homelandsecurity.com>
This comprehensive site offers profiles of terrorist groups, timelines of terrorist activity, and more.

U.S. Department of State Counterterrorism Office
<http://www.state.gov/s/ct>
This site, maintained by the U.S. government, provides information on terrorist groups and their activities.

INDEX

ABOUT THE AUTHOR

Samuel M. Katz is an expert in the field of international terrorism and counterterrorism, military special operations, and law enforcement. He has written more than twenty books and dozens of articles on these subjects, as well as creating documentaries and giving lectures. Mr. Katz also serves as editor in chief of *Special Ops*, a magazine dedicated to the discussion of special operations around the world, and observes counterterrorism and special operations units in action in Europe and the Middle East. The Terrorist Dossiers series is his first foray into the field of nonfiction for young people.

SOURCE NOTES

p. 34 David Hirst, *The Gun and the Olive Branch: The Roots of Violence in the Middle East* (London: Futura Publications Limited, 1977), 311.

PHOTO ACKNOWLEDGMENTS